The Tip of the Iceberg

Managing the Hidden Forces That Can Make or Break Your Organization

by David Hutchens

illustrated by Bobby Gombert

PEGASUS COMMUNICATIONS, INC.

Waltham

The Tip of the Iceberg:
Managing the Hidden Forces That Can Make or Break Your Organization
by David Hutchens; illustrated by Bobby Gombert
Copyright © 2001 by David Hutchens
Illustrations © Bobby Gombert

Library of Congress Cataloging-in-Publication Data
Hutchens, David, 1967–
The tip of the iceberg: managing the hidden forces
that can make or break your organization /
by David Hutchens; illustrated by Bobby Gombert. –1ˢᵗ ed.
p. cm. – (Learning fables series)
ISBN 1-883823-51-X

1. Organizational learning. 2. Management.
3. Creative ability in business. I. Title
HD58.82.H88 2001   658.4'06
QBI01-701028

Acquiring editor: Ginny Wiley
Project editors: Janice Molloy and Kali Saposnick
Editors: Lauren Keller Johnson and Kellie Wardman O'Reilly
Production: Nancy Daugherty
Marketing: Rod Williams

♲ Printed on recycled paper.
Printed in the United States of America.
First edition. First printing October 2001.

The Tip of the Iceberg
Volume Discount Schedule

1–4 copies $19.95 each	50–149 copies $13.97 each
5–19 copies $17.96 each	150–299 copies $11.97 each
20–49 copies $15.96 each	300+ copies $ 9.98 each

Prices and discounts are subject to change without notice.

Orders and Payments Offices:
PO Box 2241
Williston, VT 05495 USA
Phone: (800) 272-0945 / (802) 862-0095
Fax: (802) 864-7626
E-mail: customerservice@pegasuscom.com

Editorial and Administrative Offices:
One Moody Street
Waltham, MA 02453-5339
Phone: (781) 398-9700
Fax: (781) 894-7175
E-mail: info@pegasuscom.com

www.pegasuscom.com

06 05 04 03 02 01   10 9 8 7 6 5 4 3 2 1

5460

*For mom and dad,
who encouraged this nonsense*

Chapter 1:
A Mysterious
Chain of Events

This is the story
of a mysterious chain of events …

... that occurred far away,
on a big, jagged iceberg.

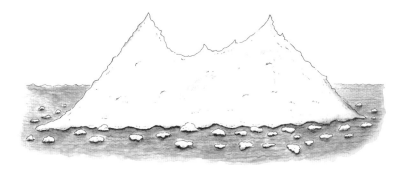

Not *that* chain of events.

This one has to do with the complex connections among some penguins …

… and clams …

… and walruses.

Before we begin the story, there are a few things you should understand.

First, penguins love to eat clams.[1]

Second, clam beds lie deep beneath the surface of the water, on the ocean floor.

[1] Don't worry—unlike the other anthropomorphized characters in this story, the clams have distinctly unpleasant personalities, so there's no need to feel sorry for them.

The penguins in this story lived on an iceberg that floated in the icy waters near the North Pole.

The resourceful little penguins knew about the clam bed that lay deep beneath them and often dreamed of eating the juicy shellfish. But, being small birds with tiny lungs, they simply couldn't hold their breaths long enough to dive all the way down to retrieve them.

Walruses eat clams, too.

With their big, strong lungs and powerful flippers, walruses have no trouble at all diving to the great depths required to reach clam beds. Plus, their tusks are ideal for prying open the hard shells.

A small pack of walruses lived just a few miles away from the penguins, on the mainland. They envied the little birds for their abundant reserves of clams.

Still, being humble and honest creatures, they respected the penguins' territory.

Hungrily, they kept their distance—though they always kept an eye open for possibilities.

So, for those of you who weren't paying close attention, here's the recap:

- The penguins had an untapped resource.

- The walruses had the procurement technology.

Perhaps you can see where this is going.

The penguins thought they did, too.
But they were wrong.

Chapter 2:
The
Penguin-Walrus
Protocol

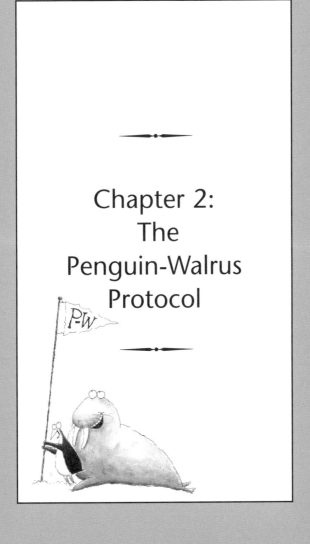

The idea of a penguin-walrus partnership had been brewing for some time and, after one particularly harsh winter, the penguins were ready to take action.

"There's a better life than this," said Sparky the penguin to the others, as his stomach grumbled loudly. "All winter long we've been living wing-to-beak. Instead, we should be feasting on clams!"

The others nodded.

"I think it's time we approached the walruses," he continued. "Agreed?"

The penguins bobbed their heads.

So negotiations with the walruses commenced. Soon, the two parties reached an agreement.

On one balmy morning as the temperature on the iceberg skyrocketed to 15 degrees below zero, the penguins invited a couple of the walruses over for a public reception to seal their new collaboration.

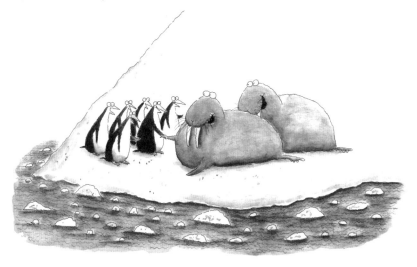

A great cheer went up from the penguins as the two walruses Gunther and Schwein heaved their massive bodies out of the water and flopped onto the iceberg.

"This is a historic day for our little iceberg," announced Sparky, trying to sound historic.

"Yes," grunted Gunther, whose eyes didn't quite work together. "This is a great day for cooperation among mammals everywhere." A low murmur arose in the crowd as some of the penguins debated whether they were, in fact, mammals.

As the eager crowd listened, Sparky read aloud the terms of their new partnership. It said

The Penguin-Walrus Protocol

1. Walruses will harvest clams for penguins.

2. In return, penguins will extend all-you-can-eat clam privileges to walruses.

3. Walruses will not eat the penguins.[2]

[2] The walruses agreed to this last clause only after tense, last-minute negotiations, prompted by an incident in which several penguins had to pry open Schwein's mouth and remove a small, discombobulated penguin.

Thundering cheers rose from the crowd as the walruses and penguins placed a flag at the edge of the iceberg to commemorate the signing of the Protocol.

Everyone was silent for a moment. Then someone said:

"What are we waiting for? Let's eat!"

And that's what they did.

Chapter 3:
Don't Mess
with Success

The Protocol proved a huge success.

Gunther, Schwein, and a couple other walruses delivered flipperloads of clams from deep beneath the iceberg to the salivating penguins, and easily pried open the shells with their tusks.

(Gunther even discovered a few pearls in the process, but, unaware of their value—or the well-worn adage—carelessly cast them before Schwein.)

Everyone had plenty to eat. The walruses freely exercised Clause 2 of the Protocol by stuffing themselves silly.

Soon, the penguins were making clam casserole. Clam soup. Clam daiquiris.[3]

Word soon spread, and penguins from other icebergs began to show up, eager to enjoy the good eating that the Penguin-Walrus Protocol had made possible.

[3] Toss clams in blender. Add ice, strawberries, and rum. Blend on high. Add mint sprig for garnish, and serve chilled.

As more and more penguins arrived, Sparky suggested that the penguins hold a Protocol Committee meeting. (This sort of thing happens in the wild more often than you would think.)

"Do we have enough clams to feed everyone who's showing up?" he asked the others who had gathered.

"Are you kidding?" said Helsinki, a little penguin with a "Type A" personality who enjoyed flaunting her expertise. "We could feed a crowd a hundred times as big as this—and still have clams left over. All we need are a few more walruses to bring up more clams."

"Okay, good," Sparky agreed. "But do we have enough room on our iceberg for everyone who's coming?"

Juneau, a penguin who had a penchant for numbers, quickly scratched some calculations in the ice. "The way I figure it," he said, "we could fit a hundred times as many as this—and still have space left over."

It was unanimous: The penguins would recruit more walruses to help meet the rising demand for clams.

So more walruses came.

They hauled more clams to the surface.

More penguins showed up.

So even more walruses came.

They hauled more clams to the surface.

And more penguins showed up.

And even more walruses came …

You get the idea.

Sparky, Juneau, and Helsinki observed all of this activity from a peak at the top of the iceberg. "This is great," Sparky grinned. "Everything seems to be working out. For once, our little colony is seeing some prosperity."

"Yes, and I attribute our success to the clams," proclaimed Helsinki.

"It does seem that the clams have made this all possible," agreed Juneau.

"Yes, and the *walruses* made the *clams* possible," Sparky added. "It's all connected."

Juneau found himself busily scratching an image into the ice as Sparky spoke. "That's an interesting point," he said after a moment. "You could draw the connections like this":

"The more *walruses* we recruit, the more *clams* we get, and the more *penguins* come."

Helsinki and Sparky were intrigued. "Yes, but don't forget," Sparky said, "then we recruit more walruses and the cycle starts all over again."

"Good point," said Juneau. He modified his drawing to look like this:

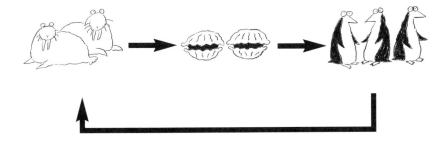

Everyone reflected silently on this exciting, spiraling dynamic: *Good things lead to more good things, which lead to even more good things—and it all gets bigger and bigger.*

But something was bothering Sparky. "How big is this going to get?" he asked, shuffling his webbed feet nervously. "Isn't this all going to have to stop eventually? The clams will run out one of these days, won't they?"

"Someday," said Helsinki. "But not for many, many years. I already told you, we have more than enough food to last us for a very long time."

"And more than enough space," reminded Juneau.

"Don't mess with success," Helsinki concluded.

"Yes," Juneau chimed in. "Don't mess with success."

After repeating this catchy little phrase a few more times, they stopped worrying.

But something was still bothering Sparky. He just couldn't put his flipper on it.

Chapter 4:
Strip Malls
and
Tanning Booths

All the penguins and walruses enjoyed the prosperity and fine dining at the iceberg, and the word kept spreading farther and farther.

More penguins showed up.

More walruses came.

More clams were brought up to the surface.

More penguins showed up.

More walruses came.

And more clams were brought up to the surface.

More penguins showed up …

Again, you get the idea.

One day, a walrus sat on a penguin.

Other than the penguin, no one took much notice.

After all, the iceberg had become a popular destination for penguins and walruses from miles around. It teemed with clam bars, strip malls,[4] and happy, well-fed crowds.

No doubt about it, it was paradise. (Unless you find the lingering smell of walrus and penguin combined with subfreezing temperatures distasteful, in which case you probably wouldn't go so far as to call it paradise. Still, you'd have to agree it was a really, *really* nice place.)

---

[4] These malls featured multiple tanning salons, a chain of yogurt shops called "I Can't Believe It's Another Yogurt Shop," and even a quaint flower boutique, owned and operated by Schwein.

But over time, certain members of the penguin population began to look a little, well, *compressed.*

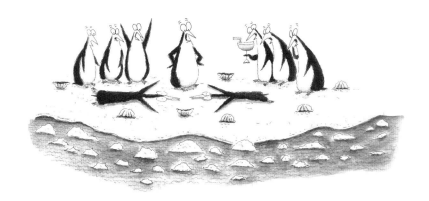

"Say, Winnipeg," Sparky said one day to a bright young penguin who was passing by. "What happened to those penguins over there?"

"Oh, that," said Winnipeg. "Some walruses sat on them."

"Why?" asked Sparky.

"Hmm, I don't know. I guess the penguins were in the wrong place at the wrong time. It's just a random thing that happens."

"Yes, well, it's not acceptable," Sparky said. "Please put out a memo: 'From now on, all walruses are to watch their back ends.' Okay?"

This Winnipeg did.

But things got worse.

As more and more penguins and walruses flocked to the iceberg, reports of penguin-flattenings increased. Sparky began to wonder whether this was indeed a "random thing."

Soon, territorial skirmishes began breaking out between walruses and penguins.

There were even reported incidents of walruses glaring at penguins, salivating and making offensive smacking sounds with their lips. (Even though this was not, legally speaking, a direct infraction of Clause 3 of the Protocol, such taunting certainly violated the spirit of the law.)

The penguins sent out more and more urgent memos, advising everyone to be more careful.

Even Sparky had a close call when a walrus sat on him, partially entrapping him under a landslide of rippling flesh.

"Why is this happening?" Sparky grunted, as Helsinki and Juneau carefully freed him from the layers of blubber. "Are you *sure* there's enough room on the iceberg for everyone?"

"I'm *certain*," Juneau insisted. "I told you before, we can fit many, *many* times more penguins and walruses. Look, I did the math. Numbers don't lie."

"Listen," said Helsinki, trying to comfort Sparky. "I really don't think this is connected to how many of us there are. This is a matter of manners and good citizenship, and everyone just needs to be reminded of that. Let me take care of this, okay?"

And so with great effort and expense, Helsinki brought in a high-priced management consultant named Hans and urged every penguin and walrus to attend his sensitivity-training workshop.

But the fighting only got worse.

As word spread around the region about the social upheaval on the iceberg, penguins and walruses stopped coming.

In fact, some of the iceberg's longtime residents were talking of packing up and leaving.[5]

Schwein, discouraged by the ill will, closed his flower shop and dived off the edge, marking a sad farewell to the days of Schwein and roses.

---

[5] Hans the consultant also jumped off the iceberg. In the process, he whacked his skull on the edge and damaged the part of the brain that allows consultants to force-fit training solutions without first doing a root-cause analysis. Hans has since recovered nicely and has joined a community of peace-loving tree-dwellers somewhere in California, where he changed his name to " ♃ ".

The little penguins called an emergency meeting near one of the iceberg's craggy peaks.

"I just don't understand it," said Winnipeg. "We're doing all the same things we did before. But now everything is going wrong!"

"We were growing quickly," Juneau added, as he doodled another diagram in the ground. "Then it all slowed down, and now we're hardly growing at all."

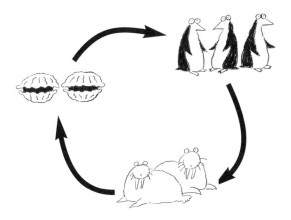

Helsinki stared at the diagram on the ground. "I think there's something missing from our picture," she said finally.

"What is it?" the others asked.

"I don't know," she said. "Some other connection. Something we can't see."

"Helsinki is right," Sparky said. "There's something else at work here. It's kind of like this iceberg. The tip is visible, and that's where you can see things happening. But the biggest part of the iceberg is invisible, under water. Maybe it's the things we *can't* see that have made everything turn bad."

Everyone fell silent. It was quiet except for the howl of the arctic wind and the distant, awful squishing sound of a walrus sitting on a penguin.

"I guess the only way things are going to get better is if we figure out what it is *we can't see,*" concluded Helsinki.

"That doesn't make sense" said Winnipeg. "How can you see something that you can't see?"

"I don't know," admitted Helsinki.

"Let's spend some time thinking about this," Sparky suggested.

The penguins went their separate ways, each lost in thought.

Obviously, penguins and walruses are territorial creatures, thought Winnipeg. *So it's natural that we would fight. But why did it suddenly start happening* now?

I wonder if we're eating too many clams, mused Helsinki. *Maybe our moods would improve with one of those low-mollusk/high-protein diets …*

This is a huge iceberg, thought Juneau. *There's plenty of space, so there's no reason for fighting. Why can't everyone just spread out some more?*

Meanwhile, Sparky had wandered to the outer edge of the iceberg, where he pondered the question that had been nagging at him all along:

Have we somehow done this
to ourselves?

Sparky threw a small chunk of ice into the calm water and watched it splash. The concentric rings of ripples spread out wider and wider, and then faded away. After a very long time, the water became still again.

Maybe whenever we do one thing, he thought, *it makes lots of other things happen—like the ripples in the water.*

Maybe it's all connected. If only we could see those connections, we could figure out ahead of time what might happen whenever we do something …

As Sparky sat and thought, he fixed his eyes on the flag that marked the historic signing of the Protocol.

It had been a long time since Sparky had looked at the flag. Something seemed funny about it. But what?

Sparky stared at it for a long moment, concentrating …

And then—

"Ah ha!" he exclaimed.

Hardly able to contain himself, he waddled furiously to find the other penguins.

Chapter 5:
The Intervention

"Everybody! Come here!" Sparky called. Juneau, Winnipeg, and Helsinki came running and sliding, tripping over each other.

"Look!" Sparky pointed at the flagpole. "What's different about the flag?"

Everybody stared blankly.

"The flag is partly under water!" Sparky yelled.

"I don't get it … " said Winnipeg. "Is it high tide or something?"

"No, silly," said Helsinki. *"The iceberg must be sinking!"*

"Yes!" added Juneau. "But why?" He thought hard for a moment. "Could it be the weight of all of these extra penguins and walruses?"

"That's it!" shouted Sparky. "*Now* I see why everyone is being so territorial. There's not as much room to spread out as there used to be. The sinking iceberg is forcing everyone too close together!"

The penguins began waddling about and honking excitedly.

Juneau rushed to scratch a new diagram in the ice. It looked similar to the original, but with one addition:

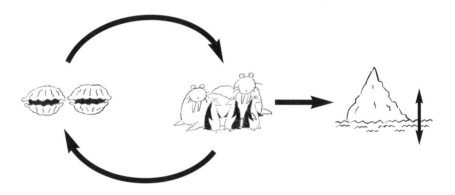

Juneau explained: "As the walruses brought more clams up, more penguins and walruses wanted to come here. And, as more penguins and walruses came, the iceberg began to sink."

"Yes, but don't forget," added Sparky, "that once the iceberg started sinking, *that* made us all start fighting—which caused folks to stop wanting to come here. Really, the picture should look like *this.*"

Sparky modified the diagram.

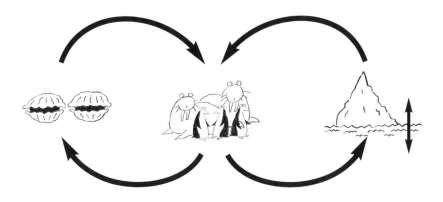

Helsinki thought hard about this seemingly simple illustration. "There's a limit to how many penguins and walruses can live on the iceberg."

"It's almost as if the iceberg has been trying to tell us that," mused Winnipeg. "We just haven't been listening."

"In fact, we've actually made things worse by recruiting more and more walruses," Juneau added. "That's why things turned ugly."

Winnipeg's comment about the iceberg caught Sparky's attention. *It's almost as if the iceberg was trying to tell us that.*

Of course, icebergs don't talk. And yet, now that Sparky thought about it, it did seem as if everything that was happening around them had been saying, "Slow down."

"It's all connected," he whispered.

"So, now that we know all this," said Winnipeg, "what do we do?"

Sparky thought carefully. "Maybe we should first agree on what we *want* to happen. Then, we can decide what we need to do to help it happen."

Helsinki added, "We also need to get better at noticing what's happening around us. Listen to the iceberg. Think about the connections between things."

Juneau was excited. "Yes," he said, "and before we do anything new, we should try to think through some of the different things that could happen as a result. We don't want to cause another disaster!"

Of course. It all seemed so obvious now.

And so, after some discussion, everyone agreed on the outcome they wanted: "To nurture our rich supply of delicious clams and make them available to all arctic creatures."

They brainstormed ideas for spreading some of the walruses and penguins to other locations, to reverse the sinking of the iceberg. (Ideas included "create a shuttle system to deliver clams to other icebergs" and "experiment with establishing new clam beds near the mainland.")

The bright little penguins even listed possible ecological and sociological impacts of these actions and formed backup plans.

Then they put it all in a PowerPoint presentation and explained it to the others. (This sort of thing happens quite frequently in the wild, due to the falling costs of digital-projection technology.)

After some group discussion, they chose a plan: to experiment with planting new clam beds near the mainland, which—unlike the iceberg—probably wouldn't sink.

They even developed a web presence with e-commerce capabilities so that penguins from all over the world could order clams. Within a few months, "Klamz.com" made its online debut.

This all marked the beginning of an exciting era for penguin-walrus relations.

Some months later, a satisfied Sparky climbed once again to the tip of the penguins' iceberg—a perfect place to reflect and to practice this new way of seeing the world.

It's a good thing we acted when we did, he thought. *I wonder what would have happened if things on the iceberg had gone on longer. Might it have been too late to save?*

Sparky then turned his attention to the bustle of activity all about him. *There must be other connections we're not seeing,* he mused. *Maybe even millions of them.*

How will our new thoughts and behaviors affect our iceberg?

How are the plans that we're putting into place now creating new results that we don't know about?

He would find out soon enough.

The
End

A Closer Look at *The Tip of the Iceberg*

Now it's your turn: Pause for a moment and consider the world around you. What are the things *you* can't see? What do you suppose are the unseen connections—between people, things, events, thoughts—that influence your world?

Like Winnipeg, you may have noticed that this question has a built-in contradiction: How can you know what you don't see if you can't see it? Fair enough. That's what this story is for. *The Tip of the Iceberg* is an *allegory* (a story filled with symbols and metaphors that communicate certain truths) designed to illuminate a new way of thinking that can help reveal some of those unseen connections and their effects.

In keeping with the allegorical approach, it is entirely appropriate to conclude that *we are not so different from the penguins.* The challenges they faced are the same ones we face every day. Maybe you sensed the penguins' frustration as they were seemingly held prisoner by forces that they couldn't see or understand. And perhaps you shared their confusion when their efforts to change things produced no results—other than to make things worse.

Reflect on your own experiences, and you will probably find similar instances of frustration, such as:

- pouring energies into well-intentioned and exhausting efforts that produce little change;

- implementing solutions *today* that produce new and more complex problems *tomorrow*;

- championing an initiative in an organization that gets off to a great start but then loses energy—and eventually fizzles; and

- pushing harder and harder to get the things you want, only to see them become less and less attainable.

As the penguins discovered, experiences like these often have roots tracing back to unseen connections. Learn to recognize those connections, and you'll see new possibilities for change.

A World of Systems

Let's get just a little more technical. All of this discussion about clams, penguins, and hidden connections is really a doorway to a fascinating body of thought known as *systems thinking*.

Systems thinking provides a whole new way of seeing that helps us understand the complex patterns of cause and effect in our world. It's a way of recognizing how things, people, and events connect to each other. For organizations, systems thinking offers rich benefits. It helps us anticipate the unintended consequences of our actions, find the highest leverage points for focusing our energy and resources, discover the underlying causes that drive our own and others' behavior, and make better decisions. From a strategic point of view, systems thinking helps us better grasp what *is* (our "current reality") so that we can design wiser strategies for creating what *can be* (our desired future).

So what is a system anyway? Here's one definition: *A system is any group of interacting, interrelated, and interdependent parts that form a complex and unified whole with a specific purpose.* The most important idea to remember is that the parts are *interacting*. If the parts aren't interacting, you don't have a system, only a bunch of things or a collection of parts.

Consider these examples of systems. Reflect on how each is composed of interacting, interrelated, and interdependent parts:
- an ant colony
- your car's engine
- your eye
- a couple playing tennis
- your marriage

- the society on the penguins' iceberg
- your organization

Can you sense how each of these systems has interacting parts and serves a specific purpose?

Now compare those systems to the following:
- a bowl of pennies sitting in your dresser drawer
- a database archived on a CD-ROM
- a wall of stacked stones
- paintings hanging in an art gallery

These latter examples are not systems; they are groups of parts. The pennies, data, rocks, and paintings do not (for all practical purposes) interact with each other. They just sit there. (If you're like many people, that bowl of pennies sits there for years!)

One fascinating aspect of systems theory is that patterns we can observe in one realm—such as an arctic ecosystem—can also occur in another, such as the human body or an organization. So it's not surprising that systems theory attracts thinkers from many different disciplines, such as the life sciences, sociology, psychology, and organizational theory. By learning to recognize certain systemic dynamics in one realm, you can begin to see them in others, too.

Intrigued? Then let's take the next step and dig a little deeper.

Some Systems Basics

To understand systems better, let's spend a few minutes exploring some of their distinguishing characteristics.

1. A system has a purpose.
2. The parts combine in a particular way for the system to carry out its purpose.
3. Systems serve specific purposes within larger systems.
4. Systems seek stability.
5. Systems have feedback.

1. A system has a purpose. One thing all systems have in common is that each has a specific *purpose*. That is, every system exists for a particular reason and is designed to *do* a specific thing. If it doesn't have a purpose, it's not a system. In the story, the purpose of the penguin-walrus partnership was to make a new source of food available to both groups. Now consider your digestive system; its purpose is to break down food so that your body can use the nutrition. Every organization is designed around a core purpose, too—one that lies deeper than the obvious drive to self-perpetuate by generating a profit. The Home Depot's purpose is to empower professionals and do-it-yourselfers in home improvement. Caterpillar manufactures heavy-duty machines, engines, and support services to "build the world's infrastructure." Internet giant Cisco Systems creates solutions to connect computer networks with people. In each case, the *purpose* drives how the organization is structured.

Here's an intriguing thought: You are a living system. So doesn't it follow that you, too, would have a unique purpose? Sure it does, although when it comes to systems that are alive, discerning purpose can be a little more difficult. (Note: The subject of individual purpose is explored in depth in the Learning Fable titled *The Lemming Dilemma: Living with Purpose, Leading with Vision,* Pegasus Communications, 2000.)

2. The parts of a system combine in a particular way for the system to carry out its purpose. Anyone who has dissected a frog in high school biology knows that a frog without a liver or a stomach is a dead frog. Likewise, remove a few gears from a clock, the cello from a string quartet, the keyboard from your computer, the shared trust in a marriage, or the marketing function from your organization, and you stunt the system's ability to carry out its function. (On the other hand, if you were to pick out all the cashews from a bowl of mixed nuts, you would not alter the functionality of the bowl of nuts. That's because a bowl of nuts is not a system, and it's not dependent on any one element, or nut.)

3. Systems serve specific purposes within larger systems. This is where systems thinking starts to get interesting. Systems are embedded within larger systems. Each maintains its own purpose while working with others to serve the larger purpose. Consider your car's ignition system. It is embedded within the larger system that is your car. *The purpose of the ignition system* is to initiate the complex mechanical and electrical processes that set the car's engine in motion. *The purpose of the car itself* is to transport the occupant (you) from one place to another. You can see how the purpose of the ignition system supports and contributes to the purpose of the car. The fact is, no system exists unconnected from the rest of the world; each is in synergistic relationship with a larger system.

It can get pretty complex. You are a system, right? And you exist in the system that is your family, which is part of your community, which is part of your society, which is part of the human race, which is part of the ecosystem of life on our planet. Actions or disturbances in any one of these systems can have ripple effects that extend up and down to other systems, with possible consequences in every connecting system.

4. Systems seek stability. You probably have a thermostat in your living room positioned at a desired setting—say, 72 degrees Fahrenheit. As the temperature outside increases or decreases, your thermostat makes adjustments—resulting in additional cold or hot air being delivered through the vents in the room. As a result of all these adjustments, the room remains a stable and comfortable 72 degrees.

This stabilizing tendency characterizes all systems. Each system has a "setting" where it "likes" to be. It will always try to return to this setting, despite external influences that seek to move it elsewhere. You can be thankful for this the next time your body fights off a virus and returns to its normal 98.6 degrees temperature. However, this stabilizing tendency also translates into the resistance to change that has given heartburn to so many managers, parents, policy makers, and so on. For instance, family systems theorists have observed that when an alcoholic father takes positive steps to conquer his addiction, other family members may subtly and subconsciously sabotage the effort because it represents a disruption to the family's established way of being. Even simple organizational initiatives—say, the introduction of a new business process—can encounter crushing resistance. That's because the new initiative produces ripples of change in a system (and its subsystems) that is seeking stability.

In the story, the penguins tried a couple of unsuccessful interventions—first a series of memos, then sensitivity training—to fix things. These measures didn't work. We all face the temptation to manipulate change by turning the most obvious "knobs." But in systems, the most obvious intervention may not always be the most enduring. Such efforts are usually about as effective as kicking a waterbed: You may see some initial movement, but eventually everything will return to its previous state.

5. *Systems have feedback.* One theorist defined systems elegantly and succinctly when he said, "A system is anything that talks to itself." His definition points to the central role of feedback in systems. Feedback refers to any information or data that returns to its source and alters a system. The thermostat's reading of your living room temperature is feedback to your home's ventilation system. The increasing fighting between penguins and walruses was feedback, too. Consider the searing sensation of pain when you bite into a much-too-hot slice of cheese pizza: that's feedback from your central nervous system. A child's increasing aggression/apathy/depression is feedback well worth listening to; so is a sudden and surprising drop in organizational productivity or a surge in sales.

If a system is healthy, it will "hear" the feedback and respond. Dysfunction and disorder occur when a system is unable to accurately recognize, interpret, or act on the feedback. The penguins believed that the infighting was an isolated phenomenon and couldn't imagine how it might be connected to their other actions. Initially, they were unable to recognize the feedback; until they did, they were unable to take relevant action.

63

From Linear Thinking to Systems Thinking

The events around us are more complicated than they appear. Often, they have many causes. Most of us know this. And yet we all face the temptation to explain things through overly simple explanations of cause and effect:

- "My marriage failed because my husband was a workaholic."

- "If we got rid of all that violent rap music, we wouldn't have this problem with street gangs."

- "Unemployment in our city is finally down, so we should definitely re-elect the mayor."

- "If they had given me a bigger budget for development, the new product launch would have succeeded."

- "If we want the fighting to stop, we should have sensitivity training."

These are all examples of *linear thinking,* in which we use "A causes B" as our model of reality. (Remember when Juneau drew the straight arrow in the ice, from the "Walruses" to the "Clams"? That's classic linear thinking.) Linear thinking is attractive because it's nice and

A Linear View

simple (and great fodder for soundbites in political elections). The problem is, it rarely reflects the complexity of the *multiple* cause-and-effect links that create our reality.

Yes, A affects B. But, as Juneau indicated in his revised diagram, B also simultaneously affects A, not to mention X, Y, and Z. So, *does* violent rap music glorify street gang culture? Did Joe's workaholism play a role in the failure of his marriage to Jane? Did the mayor's policies contribute to the decrease in unemployment? Possibly. Maybe even probably. But a systems thinker would assume *numerous* other complex factors at work in each of these scenarios. Isolating

A Systems View

one to the exclusion of the others produces a lopsided view of reality and leads us to take ineffective—or even disastrous—actions.

In the story, the walruses' actions affected the availability of clams. The availability of clams affected the attractiveness of the iceberg and, thus, the number of penguins and walruses who came. At the same time, the combined number of walruses and penguins affected the level of the iceberg in the water, which in turn influenced the fighting that broke out. The fighting made the iceberg less attractive and caused penguins and walruses to stop coming. And there were plenty of other connections we haven't even identified. Ultimately, all of these relationships and actions circled back to create important consequences for the penguins and walruses.

How do we sort through all of this complexity so that we can take effective actions and create the results we desire? Let's examine some common systemic behaviors and see if we can identify some answers for our own organizations.

Systemic Building Blocks

There are really just two basic processes that drive all activity in systems. They are *reinforcing processes* and *balancing processes*.

Reinforcing processes enhance change with even *more* change in the same direction. These processes can produce exponential growth as well as collapse. The phenomenon of compounding interest in your savings account is one simple example. Interest is generated on the balance in the account, which produces more interest, which increases the balance, which produces more interest … you get the idea. So is interest always a good thing? It depends. If the interest is working *for* you, as in your retirement account, it is. But the same dynamic can be painful if you owe more and more interest on your credit card. When the reinforcing process is positive, it is termed a "virtuous cycle." When it's negative, it's a "vicious cycle."

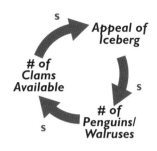

A Reinforcing Process

In the story, the penguins entered a virtuous reinforcing process in which the rate of incoming penguins and walruses increased the number of clams available for consumption, which increased the appeal of the iceberg, which further increased migration of penguins and walruses, and so on. In marketing parlance, this is the desirable "word-of-mouth" effect.

Notice how each of these variables in our reinforcing process is illustrated in the circular diagram above, where one event affects another, which affects another, and so on. This visual representation is part of a valuable systems thinking tool that we'll explore in more detail in a few moments. But for now, notice the small "s" labels (as well as the "o" labels in the following diagram). The purpose of these is to show how one variable affects another. An "s" indicates that when one variable increases or decreases, it causes the next variable to increase or decrease in the same direction as well. Thus, as the appeal of the iceberg increases, the number of penguins/walruses increases as well. An "o" means that the next variable changes in the opposite direction.

Still following? Good. (Have you noticed how systems thinking adds a powerful language and structure to things that you already suspected intuitively?) In the story, the penguins wondered why things turned bad when they did. Sparky was on to something early in the story when he wondered how long the good eating and fun could continue. In fact, every reinforcing process has some implicit limit. Nothing can grow forever. Sparky's intuition was alerting him to the other building block of systemic behavior: *balancing processes*.

Balancing processes work to keep a system at a certain level of performance. In this case, there was only a certain weight the iceberg could bear before sinking. As penguins and walruses continued to migrate to the iceberg, the actual weight of the population approached the iceberg's limit. As the iceberg sank, the amount of space on it decreased and the territorial infighting increased. News of the upheaval discouraged additional newcomers from coming, so the population leveled off—just as a thermostat brings a room back to 72 degrees.

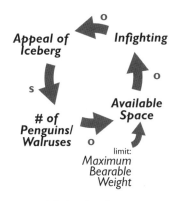

A Balancing Process

The success of a shopping mall levels out as available parking is stretched to its limit; a romantic relationship stalls as one partner encounters his or her threshold for intimacy; regional sales for a product flatten as the market becomes saturated. Each of these represents a balancing process that prevents the system from growing past a certain level.

Although balancing loops are all around you, they tend to be harder to spot than reinforcing loops. After all, it's pretty obvious when something is exponentially growing or spiraling down, right? But the balancing mechanisms that work to keep things the way they are tend to be fairly invisible. As the penguins discovered, identifying and understanding these hidden balancing processes is a major key to managing change in your organization, or in any other system.

Looping It Together

Perhaps you've noticed that our loops look similar to the ones that Juneau scratched in the ice. Like the penguins, we are now using a systems thinking tool known as *causal loop diagramming*. Causal loop diagramming is just one of several visual languages for illustrating the dynamics of systems.

Now let's put our two drawings—the reinforcing loop and the balancing loop—together in a more dynamic causal loop diagram to consider what happens when the two interact. Here's where things start to get really interesting:

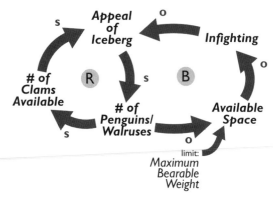

A Causal Loop Diagram of the Iceberg System

Notice that, in addition to joining the two loops together, this picture includes a couple of extra details. In the center of the left loop, there is an "R," and in the right loop a "B." These are just helpful reminders that the left loop is a *reinforcing* one and the right one is a *balancing* one. Remember, no matter how complex they become, systems are always composed of some combination of just these two basic building blocks.

Now let's "read" our causal loop diagram for a big-picture understanding of the dynamics of the iceberg system.[1] We'll walk through it one step at a time.

Start at the bottom center of the diagram with the variable that says "# of Penguins/Walruses." As the number of penguins and walruses increases, the *number of clams available for consumption* increases, too. As the number of available clams increases, the *appeal of the iceberg* also increases. Positive word of mouth causes the *number of penguins and walruses* to increase. As the number of penguins/walruses

---

[1] Some people consider causal loop diagrams and other visual representations of systems overly simple because they don't capture the myriad complexity of any given system. Their point is well taken. Some of the richest representations of systems come from dynamic and detailed computer models that can better depict a system's true complexity. A causal loop diagram is best thought of as a *simplified snapshot* of our *current understanding* of systemic forces in a *certain context*. Kept in its proper perspective, these diagrams can illuminate certain valuable insights, as you're about to discover. So, with respect for their limitations, let's forge ahead.

increases, the number of available clams increases even further, and so on. Our reinforcing process is escalating nicely in a virtuous cycle.

Now let's loop over to the right side. As the number of penguins/walruses continues to increase, their combined weight approaches the iceberg's limit. This weight causes the iceberg to begin to sink, and the *amount of available space* decreases. With less space per animal, the amount of *territorial infighting* increases, which reduces the appeal of the iceberg to other penguins.

Finally, let's complete our trip with a return to our reinforcing loop on the left. With the appeal of the iceberg now *decreasing*, the number of penguins and walruses begins to decrease. In turn, the number of available clams decreases as well, because there aren't as many walruses to harvest them, which further hurts the appeal of the iceberg, and so on. Growth on the iceberg has now halted. The reinforcing process is no longer a virtuous one.

See what just happened? The penguins entered into a reinforcing process. They continued to push the system for more and more growth, mistakenly believing they were far from the system's capacity. But as they approached the system's true limit (which, to that point, they hadn't seen), the system resisted further change.

As the penguins learned, we can become trapped by systems when we fail to understand them. The more aware we become of underlying systemic structures, the more leverage for change we possess. As systems theorist Daniel H. Kim puts it, we must learn to work *on* the system as opposed to working *in* the system. Or to put it another way, Kim asks, *How can we become better* designers *of systems rather than mere* operators *of systems?*

When we are unaware of how a system works, we're reduced to reacting to the specific *events* that it produces—the visible part of the *iceberg* (*"Hey, harvesting clams makes our lives better! Therefore, we should keep harvesting clams."*). But systems thinking helps us see beyond

The Iceberg Model

events—to the *patterns* of events over time (*"I don't think these penguin-sitting incidents are just random events!"*). When we notice patterns, we're more likely to see the invisible structures driving those patterns (*"The iceberg is sinking!"*). We can then act with much more effectiveness, either by redesigning the system we are in or by creating new systems that produce the results we desire.

A Next Step: The Systems Archetypes

The Tip of the Iceberg and the causal loop diagram you just explored represent just one pattern of systems behavior. The plot of this story focused exclusively on a specific pattern in which a system reaches its growth limit. However, don't think this is the only kind of systems story that can play out. There are plenty of other stories that can be told as well. We call these stories *archetypes*.

Think of an archetype as a common storyline, a systemic drama that tends to repeat itself in many different parts of our lives. *The Tip of the Iceberg* is built on an archetype known as "Limits to Success." (Does the penguins' experience ring painfully true in your own organization? If so, then you'll want to look more deeply into the "Limits to Success" archetype.)

If you choose to continue your exploration of systems thinking beyond the penguins' iceberg experience, you'll discover other common archetypes that can reveal new insights and high-leverage interventions for any number of organizational scenarios:

- *The "Fixes That Fail" archetype* shows how quick-fix solutions that provide temporary results can also produce intense, chronic, and undesirable long-term results.

- *The "Shifting the Burden" archetype* shows how a solution implemented to alleviate a symptom results in a dependence on the solution and undermines the system's ability to resolve the deeper problem. This structure represents the pattern of behavior that also drives much *addiction*.

- *The "Escalation" archetype* occurs when two parties each perceive the other's actions as a threat, and both respond in threatening ways. The threats grow exponentially until both parties are at a standoff. This archetype is behind price wars between competing products, as well as other forms of competition.

- *The "Drifting Goals" archetype* illuminates the temptation for an organization to lower its goals rather than overcome the obstacles to achieving those goals. This is the dynamic of chronic underperformance.

- *The "Tragedy of the Commons" archetype* illustrates a scenario in which different groups draw on or compete for a limited resource. (You've experienced this if you've battled rush-hour gridlock on the highway of a major city.)

- *The "Success to the Successful" archetype* echoes sayings such as "the rich get richer and the poor get poorer." This archetype illuminates scenarios where two groups compete for a limited resource—and the one who realizes early success is likely to continue garnering the lion's share of the resource.

- *The "Growth and Underinvestment" archetype* shows what happens when growth approaches a limit that could be eliminated if the organization made capacity investments. By not making these investments, demand degrades, which leads to even fewer investments in capacity, and so on.

One great place to explore these archetypes is the Pegasus Communications workbook titled *Systems Archetype Basics.* You'll find it and other excellent titles in the *Suggested Further Reading* section at the end of this book.

Becoming a Systems Thinker

If systemic forces are so resistant to our interventions, does that mean that we have no options for change? Luckily, as human beings, we do have the capacity to reflect and learn. We have the ability—the *privilege*—to change in order to create the results we care about.

When we embrace the discipline of systems thinking, we begin to see the world very differently. To the extent that we foster our awareness of systems, we can move from a reactive stance, in which we merely respond to events, to an intentional or creative one, in which we can design systems that produce sustainable results in our organizations.

Like all skills, systems thinking is one that must be practiced before a degree of proficiency can be reached. You can begin practicing by applying the concepts and tools to your own business reality. Here are some things to think about as you begin defining a context for practicing the skills:

- Assume that your current experience or results are the product of *multiple* contributing factors—not just the one factor that is most obvious or visible to you.

- Identify small-scale problems as opportunities for applying systems thinking to achieve better results.

- Partner with someone skilled in the discipline of systems thinking or interested in exploring a systemic approach to a chronic issue.

- Seek perspectives from different parts of the system. For example, cultivate the practice of *dialogue* with representatives from different functions in the organization to gain a more complete view of the problem.

- Ask the "five whys." That is, as you seek to understand the cause of an event, ask "Why did that happen?" After identifying the cause, ask again "And why did *that* happen?" Do this a total of five times as you dig deeper and deeper to the root cause of an event.

- Start with the process of defining variables.

- Don't get too preoccupied with drawing causal loop diagrams. Any diagrams that you *do* develop should be considered your current state of understanding and not the final word.

- Be suspicious of quick fixes.

- Focus on solutions that optimize the whole, rather than each of the parts. For example, instead of saying, "How can we fix those guys over in the sales department," consider the larger context of the organization as a whole. *Then* take a fresh look at the sales department's relationship to the larger system.

- For any solution you identify, look for potential unintended side effects that may result.

- Don't bite off too much. Instead, focus on a few key changes over time.

- Expect the change process to take a while. Applying systems thinking won't solve major, chronic problems immediately.

Or, to put it even more simply: *Look. Listen. Reflect.* Then take action. You may never approach your relationship to the world the same way again.

Questions for Group Discussion

——◦——

- What was the primary system described in the story? What were the parts of that system? What was the system's purpose?

- Continue to reflect on the primary system in the story. What was the larger system in which it was embedded? What were some of its smaller "subsystems"?

- In what way did the penguins' system seek stability? How did it respond to the penguins' initial efforts to change things? Why did it respond in this way?

- Why was it hard for the penguins to recognize and diagnose the feedback in their system?

- Now think about your organization. What kinds of processes, structures, and beliefs make it difficult to recognize and respond appropriately to feedback?

Acknowledgments

Special thanks and appreciation to:

The staff of Pegasus Communications (the "Pegasi"), including *Ginny, Janice, Kali, Nancy, Rod,* and the "Pegasi-in-spirit," *Kellie* and *Laurie.* A hard day collaborating on a Learning Fable is still better than a good day doing "real work" at the office!

The reviewers. Much like using a sledgehammer to swat a fly, this text was reviewed, tested, and shaped by some of the best thinkers and practitioners in the field of systems thinking, including *Ben Bruce, LouAnn Daly, Teresa Hogan, Daniel H. Kim, Dave Packer, Patti Russell,* and *Don Seville.*

Finally, to my wife *Robbie,* my daughter *Emory,* and now *Oliver,* the newest member of the growing, living system that is the Hutchens family—a virtuous, reinforcing cycle of love, meaning, and affirmation, spiraling ever higher without end.

Suggested Further Reading

Learning Fables
Outlearning the Wolves: Surviving and Thriving in a Learning Organization
  (available in soft cover or as an e-book)
Shadows of the Neanderthal: Illuminating the Beliefs That Limit Our
  Organizations
The Lemming Dilemma: Living with Purpose, Leading with Vision

Systems Thinking for Kids
When a Butterfly Sneezes: A Guide for Helping Kids Explore Interconnections in
  Our World Through Favorite Stories
Billibonk & the Thorn Patch
Billibonk & the Big Itch

The Pegasus Workbook Series
Systems Thinking Basics: From Concepts to Causal Loops
Systems Archetype Basics: From Story to Structure

Volumes in the Innovations in Management Series
Introduction to Systems Thinking
Designing a Systems Thinking Intervention
From Mechanistic to Social Systemic Thinking: A Digest of a Talk by Russell L.
  Ackoff

Pocket Guides
Guidelines for Daily Systems Thinking Practice
The Do's and Don't's of Systems Thinking on the Job
Palette of Systems Thinking Tools
Guidelines for Drawing Causal Loop Diagrams

Other Titles by Pegasus Communications

Pegasus Anthologies
Organizational Learning at Work: Embracing the Challenges of the New Workplace
Making It Happen: Stories from Inside the New Workplace
Organizing for Learning: Strategies for Knowledge Creation and Enduring Change

The Innovations in Management Series
Concise, practical volumes on systems thinking and organizational learning
  tools, principles, and applications

Newsletter
The Systems Thinker®

Free e-bulletin
Leverage Points™ *for a New Workplace, New World* is a free e-bulletin
spotlighting innovations in leadership, management, and organizational
development. To subscribe, go to www.pegasuscom.com.

For a complete listing of Pegasus resources, visit www.pegasuscom.com.